DISTRACTORS

BREAKING FREE FROM TOXIC PEOPLE WHO KEEP YOU FROM YOUR PURPOSE

GERALDINE "GERRI" HOLMES

3G Publishing, Inc.
Loganville, Ga 30052
www.3gpublishinginc.com
Phone: 1-888-442-9637

First published by 3G Publishing, Inc. February, 2022.

ISBN: 9781941247990

Printed in the United States of America

Dedication

This book is dedicated to my husband and family.

I would like to first give a special thank you to my husband, Keith D. Holmes, Sr., my children: Ajaya Morgan, Kameisha Holmes, Kiera Holmes, Keith Holmes, Jr., and Taelor Holmes. I also want to give thanks to my Morgan Family: Elizabeth Morgan (Mother), Siblings; Jeffery Morgan, Kimberly Alexander, Craig Morgan, Kasey Morgan, and Ranji Morgan for allowing me space and time to prepare for a book that I have desired to write for years. Thank you for your patience in allowing me time to focus on something most important to me; the beginning of a journey of becoming the author of my first book. We all have our own stories, but to be able to put words inside of a book is awesome. I am forever grateful for your love and support.

To my favorite teacher Joyce Edwards Brown, who I met over 37 years ago; unknowingly, she brought me out of a dark place in my life at age 14. This teacher looked at me and saw something very SPECIAL in me. Her patience, smile, and kindness allowed me to believe in myself and gave me the drive to rise and shine.

Special GEMS In The Core

My best friend, Deanna "Dee Dee" Burley Lee, whom I

met in August 1984 at Morris Brown College. Thank you for showing me what true friendship looks like, how to communicate in love, and always showing support and respect. To my other Californian sisters; Alecia "Lee Lee" Williams and Jules Smith, thank you for embracing me into your heart and loving me as a true sister. My darling, sister-friend Carolyn Daniels, who witnessed my "falls" and "flaws", never gave up on me she knew me from the inside out.

Last, a special thank you to all my female and male affiliations who shine bright like diamonds around me:

DIVA Girls

Fun Fam

Ladies of Distinction (L.O.D.)

Loyal Girlfriends

Real Women

Soul Sistahs

Acknowledgement

All Glory and Praise to GOD for allowing me to get this message out to those who have experienced toxic people in their lives and could not see an open door. Distractors have always been in my life. Each time I would decide to stay strong and focus on my dreams, interruptions would come from who I would refer to as distractors.

Distractors can disturb your peace and ability to focus directly on your purpose. I am thankful for the many friendships I've experienced throughout my life. Good or bad, they all were a part of my writing journey for this book. You all are valuable, and I am grateful to have crossed your paths. It was your trials and tribulations that I encountered either as a friend, therapist counselor, or sister that needed my attention, either as a friend, therapist, counselor, or sister, that allowed me to see the hurt caused on you by others. Without these experiences and support from you all, this book would not exist.

I want to also thank my hairstylists Maggie and Ann Marie (DeNovo Salon), and make-up artist Nneka (IG Mua_Bvic) for their gifted hands in contributing to my "look". Your work has truly made a difference in allowing me to present my best self-image.

You have allowed me to help many people break free from toxic people and achieve their dreams. I don't take this for granted, thank you!

TABLE OF CONTENT

Introduction

Care about what other people think, and you will always be their prisoner – Lao Tzu

Twice a year, I try to put a positive message out to help someone who may need this advice. First, let me remind you, "We Are All Designed To Thrive." One of the most popular questions I'm always asked is – Gerri, how do you manage to be so happy? Allow me to share. Please understand that I have not always been in this place but I am now. I have been here for almost 20 years now. As you get older and you have many experiences with various people and relationships, you become wiser. The key to HAPPINESS is having GOD and the right type of people in your life. Folks, please understand that everyone does not belong in your circle or life.

We all know how important it is to give our bodies a break from "toxic" food and alcohol--but what about giving ourselves a break from toxic attitudes? Just like any toxic thing such as food or poison, toxic people are extremely dangerous. They distract us from our positive or productive habits. They'll be the people who discourage you from exercise or make fun of you for wanting to be a better person. They'll also come up with reasons for you to stay in other bad relationships. A toxic person's persuasion can have you stuck in your past and focused on the negative.

In that mentality, you can't move forward and you can't succeed. They can't share in your joy."

It's worth noting that there is a difference between people who are truly toxic to your well-being versus people who have a negative outlook because of their struggle with depression. For friends and family members who suffer from clinical depression, it's important to let them know that you love and support them by not cutting them out of your life. Interacting with toxic people who constantly cut you down or manipulate you to their advantage can take a toll on your mental health. There are times it can be difficult to distance yourself from them.

"Toxic people can try to cling on—sometimes for years! They try to make you feel guilty and because of that, it's not always easy to remove them from your life. Hopefully, this book will help you detox your relationships once and for all.

This book's mission is to guide you to live the best parts of your life by breaking free from toxic people without caring about what their opinions or what they have to say about you or who you are becoming. I hope it will make you understand that you have the power to steer your life in any direction you choose. As I like to say, you are the artist of your life. Life is an art. Make it your masterpiece. Please read at your leisure. It's sure to truly help anyone struggling in this area of life.

Chapter 1

Your First Friend

When we are born, we come into the world alone as individuals. It is only during growth that we begin to recognize parents, siblings, and even begin to grow a circle of friends. However, the truth is that even at birth, we are not on our own. There is someone who is with us even when it feels like we are by ourselves. We have a true friend. He is God. God is the author of all things. God is He who knows the end from the beginning. GOD is the person who knows when you are going to be born. He knows what you are going to look like and be like. He knows all life experiences that are going to befall you, and even knows when you will depart from this Earth. GOD knows who our parents are going to be even before our conception.

Aside from the fact that God cares for you and is with you, there's someone else who takes you as her responsibility as soon as your fertilization is confirmed. Your mother becomes your first friend as soon as you become an embryo. Your mother carried and cared for you for 9 months. Throughout those months, she consciously made sure she ate properly and had a balanced meal, drinks, and took the necessary vitamins for your proper growth and development. By the first time you opened your eyes, your mother was there, giving you the most amazing welcome in her arms with an undiluted joy all over her face. A mother will love you right away and look as if she will never let go.

As you begin to grow from an infant to a toddler and begin to walk and talk, you will recognize the two most important people who are there to guide you on how to eat, drink, walk, talk and keep you from falling. Your parents are there to nurture you and bear you in their hands, making sure you are sufficiently guided and safe. Just like most other people, my first true friendship was with my parents and later my siblings. It was always a feeling of sincere, genuine love, protection and safeguarding. I believe parents are naturally created to be your best friends because you are their child. A parent-child relationship is a very unique type of relationship because when you are born, your parents see no wrong in you and they will go the extra length to protect you. They will love you, treat you right and no matter what you do wrong or whatever mistakes you make, your parents will step in and protect you. Your parents allow you to be vulnerable (you can cry, hurt, be in pain, and showcase your flaws). This was the beginning of my expectations of how all people should be until I experienced my siblings.

Friendship with Siblings and Other Family Members

Your second level of friendship comes from your siblings (a brother and sister or in some cases, all brothers, all sisters or a mixture of both). GOD saw fit to create and bring me forth first as the oldest child. I have four brothers and two sisters. I truly got an opportunity to experience so many different characteristics in each of my siblings. Although we come from the same parents, all of us look different and have unique personalities. I had different relationships with each of my siblings because they were different.

As the oldest, I learned that siblings don't look at you in a caring and loving way. They are willing to compete, fight for attention from the parents, argue, fight and/or play fun games with you. During my younger years, the concern for safety was off-limits because it was all about fun. Being the oldest, I always looked out for my younger siblings. Most of the time, if you are the oldest, usually, you have to look out for yourself.

As I journeyed through my life as a kid with my siblings, I observed that although we were siblings, we also became friends. Some siblings are indeed closer than others. We defined our friendship as close-knit because we are born of the same parents. There was certainly a difference between the two relationships because I knew my Parents loved, cared, and protected me. I was able to be vulnerable. With my siblings, our friendship was different because I did not feel the same guard of protection I had with my parents.

Your siblings feel like your equal. They are willing to challenge you, debate with you and display the difference in their behavior. Being the oldest, I enjoyed the excitement of having a lot in common with my siblings. It was 9 of us (2 parents, 4 boys, and 3 girls) all living in the same house. As siblings, you learn to laugh and have fun with one another. However, you learn to fight, explore the world of jealousy, negativity, and become the sibling that is a "tattle tale" or being the sibling who loves to be sneaky and play games.

Discovering the difference with parents was an E & E (experience and education); It wasn't something you train for in life; it was an entire experience. Siblings come with an entirely new agenda of their own. I quickly discovered the difference between my parents who adored me and my siblings who tolerated me. The level of friendship was different but dealing with both prepared me for the beginning of more good/bad personalities, behavior, and disappointments to come.

Identification of Friends

Our society tend to emphasize romantic relationships. We think that finding that right person will make us happy and fulfilled. But research shows that friends are even more important to our psychological welfare. Friends bring more happiness into our lives than virtually anything else. Friendships have a huge impact on your mental health and happiness. Good friends relieve stress, provide comfort, joy, and prevent loneliness and isolation.

Developing close friendships can also have a powerful impact on your physical health. Lack of social connection may pose as much of a risk as smoking, drinking too much, or leading a sedentary lifestyle. Friends are even tied to longevity. One Swedish study found that, along with physical activity, maintaining a rich network of friends can significantly add years to your life. There's an understanding that the binding together of people in friendship helps each of us define and realize a meaningful life.

As we journey through life, we encounter and make friends at different stages of our lives. These friends play different roles in our lives and they differ in importance. Below is a detailed look into the kinds of friends we have at different stages in our lives.

Levels of Friendship

Elementary Friends

During your childhood, your mind is "child-like." You are in elementary school with other kids, and just like you, they are seeking someone to be their friend. At this age, you have no care in the world, no responsibility and your life involves playing, homework, eating, and looking for something fun to do. When I was in elementary school during recess time, just like most kids, I wanted a playmate.

It seemed that most of the kids on the playground were just happy to be outdoors. While at the playground I would always find myself gravitating to the same person for play-time. This would also happen in the school's cafeteria. Then, that's when the simple, but fun conversations would start.

During that time you start noticing everyone gather together and play. Once you start noticing the same person outside, you begin to gravitate towards them and play, which is what I did. Once you find that one person you see all the time at the playground, you start noticing them in the cafeteria and start having a simple conversation. I thought during elementary school, those friends were the beginning of a solid long-term relationship. I quickly learned that this would change. From babysitters, daycare centers to elementary school you play with one or two friends you started playing with at first. Then, you feel your first disappointment and ultimate betrayal because they want to play with others. However, you join in because you will feel as long as you are involved, you are good.

Of course, there would be times that certain kids would not want to play with you. Though the disappointment makes you sad, the disappointments quickly goes away within seconds. You gradually look forward to the next day. As a child, your friendship starts as soon as you meet others who may not be members of your school. It begins to shape the beginning of many friendships and disappointments you will experience later on in life.

Middle School Friends

When you enter middle school, peer pressure is one of the scariest things you will experience. Peer pressure is at an all-time high. Your parents have gone from being your friends to your enemies because your hormones are going crazy. You are not sure what your body is experiencing and it seems you are more irritated than ever.

During my middle school years, at home, my parents and siblings were always getting on my nerves. I soon discovered that other classmates were experiencing the same thing. This is when conversations begin about your teachers, parents, boys, girls, siblings, menstrual cycle, and sex. I started to gravitate more towards classmates with whom I had similar conversations. We would talk in the cafeteria or in the classroom. I noticed some of them from elementary school and we began to chat about the same topics. During that time, I felt excited to have someone I could talk with and call a friend.

This level of friendship seems so simple because you are building a relationship with friends that are the same as you. You both experience irritation with parents, you talk together about other classmates and have sneaky conversations about boys and sex. During this time, you truly feel like these are friends for Life.

In the 3rd year of middle school, you feel this friendship from elementary school will follow you all throughout middle school. However, you realize that you may or may not have an interest in being friends with them in middle school, and they may feel that same way about you. While in middle school, you assume that because you were elementary friends, that this would automatically translate to you being friends in middle school.

However, I started noticing some changes in my peers that I didn't recognize. I also noticed that even I started changing. Personalities were clashing to the point that you just don't want to be bothered. When I got to that point, I began to interact with new classmates. During the four years in middle school, you understand that bullying, peer pressure, and those who are or not having sex, seem to bring about two divisions.

Some of the friends you feel connected to will begin to do things that you may not agree with; which could lead to you cutting off some old friends. However, you soon discover that 2-4 friends you had in elementary school are gone and you have now connected with 3-8 new friends. Friends with who you have a lot more in common through relatable conversations and school activities. During the crisis of peer pressure, your friends are mostly still learning the definition of a friend. The experiences of understanding who they were in elementary school and now in middle school are different. You realize that some have changed or done things you are not interested in or can't do, so the level of the friendship has to change.

Realizing and deciding who your friends are will soon be discovered based on the experience together and what you have in common. You will become well aware of those you are interested in keeping in your life. Your new middle school friends are now those who will follow you over to high school.

High School Friends

Entering high school was such an exciting time for me because I understood that it was my last four years to be at home with my parents and going to some type of college/ university was at the top of my mind. After all, it's been something I've been thinking about since I was in middle school.

So, planning to move away and start a new life was a priority for me. Most of your friends feel the same way too. Your relationship with your childhood friends (middle school and high school) is at a level of respect. You've seen each other grow from being children to maturing as teens. I realized quickly that once I got to high school, it would not be a walk in the park as it was for me in elementary and middle schools.

The next four years of high school were very challenging for me. Some of my friends from elementary and middle school had changed; and I had changed. I narrowed my friendship down to 2-3 friends. I decided that I would eat lunch and be with just one of them all the time.

My bond with my friend Yvonne Gilchrist was so perfect because we had been together during middle school and now high school. For 4 years, we would walk together from the bus to classes, eat lunch together and walk back to the bus when classes end. Everyone knew us as besties; Geraldine and Yvonne.

I had gotten to know her during middle school along with others who I had known in elementary school, but as I was beginning to mature, it appeared Yvonne was already slightly mature and we just lined up together. As I continued to build more relationships with others and remain friends with my elementary and middle school peers, we all would be dealing with a new set of challenges that would not be under our control. This began to set off a change in our friendship.

As I entered my senior year, I noticed some of my friends got scholarships to go to college. Some got pregnant and dropped out of high school. Others experienced drugs/alcohol and had major problems, and a few were selected as the most popular, had cars, got summer jobs and succeeded on their way out as seniors. Due to the personality dynamic with high school friends, this would set off a chain of challenges in my friendships.

Halfway through high school, the 6-8 friends I started with began to reduce because of jealousy, hatred, challenges, addiction, and emotional offset which was out of my control. I began to consume myself with my college plans and decided to stick with someone who had the most respect for me and our friendship and that was Yvonne. There were others that I was close to, Deborah "Dee Dee" Houston, Sandra "Shel" Thurmond, Patricia "Pat" Gardenhire, Tabatha Nixon, Tammy Anderson, Victor Gilchrist, and Cheryl "Net" Leverette. Each of us came from different backgrounds, but when we got together, I only remembered the fun times I experienced with them. Nothing was short of laughter and love. Once I made up my mind that they would be the friends I would end up with, I was content and now I could focus on preparing for college.

I spent each summer talking mainly on the phone to my friends because I was under strict rules by my parents. I was not allowed to go out and do many things with my friends. The time I had with my friends in high school was somewhat limited. I knew I had to be sure what I wanted to do with my life; work part-time, work hard academically, apply to college, and research financial aid resources.

I have met, gained, and developed friendships throughout the years of school. I have gone through the ups and downs, hurt and disappointments. I definitely thought this would be the end of flaws with friends from school. Still, as I set out into the real world identifying those friends during some of the seasons in life, it was still a challenge and learning experience.

Friends - How Many of Us have Them?

In 1984, the group "Whodini"–came out with a song in the '80s titled "Friends"! How many of us have them?

I've highlighted some of the most important lines of the song that are important to me:

Friends, how many of us have them?

Friends, ones we can depend on.

Friends, how many of us have them?

Friends, before we go any further let's be friends.

If you listen to that song, it is very true and profound. As you walk the journey of learning about the various people in your lives, you will identify those who have become distractors in your lives. Distractions are not all bad, but if the people or things you are associated with do interrupt your journey to your purpose, then it can be bad.

The word distraction is not at all a bad word because sometimes you can get distracted by someone to avoid walking into a bee hive or snake. However, people in your life can constantly remain and interrupt you and cause many disruptions and delays in what you are trying to do.

A person, who understands the benefits of a friend and values it with respect, will remove themselves when they know their problem is not to continue interrupting the lives of others. If your family and friends display any toxic behavior and they are constantly interrupting your goals and preventing you from getting to your purpose, please remove yourself.

Notes

Notes

Notes

Chapter 2

Who is in Your Life?

Once you realize that your parents, siblings, and other family members are the foundation of the beginning of friendships, your view changes. Your view of your childhood friends from elementary, middle and high school, college peers, and colleagues on the job now have different relevance. During these years, you are getting to know various people, building relationships and deciding who you will maintain a short or long term relationship with. The truth is, our close relationships have a disproportionate effect on our lives for the amount of time we spend intentionally thinking about them. For most people, the closest relationships in their lives were arbitrarily chosen for them by their school system, their job, or the activities they happen to enjoy when they were teenagers. And they haven't thought about it since. They see the same people, hang out in the same places, and have the same conversations — on repeat.

What's wrong with that, you ask? Well, nothing. Allow me to reframe it for you: It isn't that something is wrong — it's that it could be exponentially better. Having long-lasting friendships is a wonderful thing. Not choosing them intentionally is a missed opportunity.

If someone offered a chance for you and a team of your choosing to go on a quest that had a prize of $10 million at the end, how carefully would you choose that team? You'd likely sit down and carefully analyze the most critical characteristics for your team to win the quest. Well, the quest is called life, and the prize at the end is worth more than $10 million.

During your quest in life, you will discover the various levels of friendships; you will experience the ups and down of hurt and disappointments from many of them. This will be the beginning of a deep dive into friendship (the one who's been there with you from the beginning that knew you as a child, the ones who come into your life as adults and you introduce them to your childhood friends and the ones you meet during your career in college and work). I begin to look around to see what types of people were in my life, what personalities, and behaviors I was dealing with. During this evaluation period, I realized the following major behaviors I endured were:

Followers

The Negative person

The bossy and controlling women

Judgmental men and women

Jealousy from both men and women

Hateful spirits; mainly from women

Each relationship with others was different because of how it made me feel. As I evaluated and dissected the feelings for each of them, I had to break them up into categories by feelings in the D's – Disappointment and Draining:

Followers: Disappointment

The Negative person: Draining

The bossy and controlling women: Draining

Judgmental men and women: Disappointment

Jealousy from both men and women: Disappointment/ Draining

Hateful spirits; mainly from women: Draining

I was starting to feel overwhelmed; I began to lose focus. My schedule was full of appointments from family and friends who were pouring a lot of their issues and problems on me, not once, but a lot. I could not stay on course with anything. The vast majority of my time, I was a mother, counselor, therapist, consultant and when it was all over, I realized I was not able to do any of the things I set out to do each day. Each year just like most, I would make my resolution of what I was going to do and what I had planned to accomplish by that year. However, after February, it seems my days, weeks, months became more about everyone else's problems and events other than my own goals. The day I may have had planned would always be interrupted by what others wanted.

Yes, my day was beginning to end up like an appointment with patients and clients at a doctor or therapist. I was beginning to realize that the years were steadily flying by and I still had not accomplished most of what I set out to do. Year after year, I would make the same resolution and/or promise to myself saying, "I must remove these toxic folks and their situations out of my life." "I must stop allowing others' needs before mine." I knew I needed to take a deeper dive into why was I attracting these type of people and why I continued to allow them to be in my life.

Putting yourself first doesn't mean you don't care about others. It means you're smart enough to know you can't help others if you don't help yourself first – Simple Reminders.

A life spent ceaselessly trying to please people who are perhaps incapable of ever being pleased, or trying too hard to always be seen as doing "what's expected of you," is a sure road to a regretful existence. Do more than just exist. We all exist. The question is: Do you want to live? Live for YOU!

People will talk. They always have and they always will. No matter what you do or say, how you behave, the way you walk or dress, how you act or the decisions you make, will always be scrutinized by others. It's the nature of the masses. Like the herd of lions swooping in for the kill, they prey on the weak, looking for those they can taunt and torment and it gets to us. We allow other people's opinions to not only hurt us but oftentimes, to define us.

It doesn't matter what other people think of you. It doesn't matter what other people say about you behind closed doors or even right in front of your face. Their opinions have no basis in defining what you're all about. They aren't the truth. They have no purpose other than to hurt or harm you. There is no rhyme or reason beyond making other people feel superior to you in some way or another. This isn't something new. Other people have always had an opinion. From early on in our lives, we form cliques.

As children, we tend to gang up on others in an effort to not only make that person feel bad, but to make ourselves feel better. Just because someone is different from you, doesn't make them inferior. No one is better than you no matter what. No matter the color of their skin, their religion, their occupation, nor anything else for that matter. No one.

Still, it's hard to not get disheartened when others hurl intentionally-hurtful opinions at you. It's easy to think in your mind that those opinions don't matter and don't define you as a human being, but it's harder to put in practice. It is considering that we've all been the target of an ill-intentioned opinion at one point or another; most of us know just how this feels. It's hard to suppress your emotions when people are doing their best just to get you going.

Still, it's important to take the high road. It's important to turn the other cheek and look the other way. Not only for your own sanity but for the simple fact that you shouldn't give others the pleasure of insulting you. You shouldn't allow their negativity to stir you into a fury. It doesn't matter what other people think. Not at all. As long as you're doing the right thing and you're interested in creating value and contributing to the world, you shouldn't care what anyone else thinks or says.

People will always find someone to talk about. Throughout history, people have always found someone to talk about. They've ganged up on those they perceived as different, or in some way a threat to their own existence. This is steeped in our society and culture, and goes back towards the dawn of modern man. Why do you torment others for no real purpose? Why do we cast out those who are different? What is it about human society that makes this something so ingrained into our lives?

The fact of the matter is that people will always find something or someone to talk about. They will always convey their opinions and cast out those who they feel are weak, misfits or simply don't "fit in" with others because they're too fat, too skinny, too dark, too white, too religious, too fanatical, too smart, too dumb, or whatever have you. At the end of the day, it doesn't matter. People will always find someone to talk about.

We don't live in a perfect world where everyone is the same, with the same set of skills or upbringings or talents. No. We live in a wide and diverse world, where genetic mutations from the dawn of time have led to an overall diversity in the species on this planet. Within every species, there are countless more diversities. The difference is that humans are conscious and aware of their existence and tend to find solace in tormenting and weakening the spirits of others.

Your self-worth isn't defined by an approval rating.No matter what the naysayers and the purveyors of negativity around you might say, your self-worth isn't defined by an approval rating. There's no objective rating scale that allows another person to judge you. They don't know what you've been through. They don't know your story, your trials, your tribulations, or the path you've walked through the shadow of the valley of death. No, it simply doesn't work that way.

However, too often, we do define our self-worth by an approval rating. We do allow what others say or think about us to influence how we feel about ourselves. The happiness barometer is often influenced by the he-said-she-said pipeline. That grapevine makes it to us in some way or another, whether electronically or verbally, and we feel the effects of that, similar to a ground-altering earthquake.

It jolts us. It sickens us. It makes us depressed. It shouldn't. But it does. We allow it to do that. And because we allow it, we stoke the fire of feelings and angst. We help to spread the conflagration of negativity when people know that it's affecting us. They know that pressing that button is going to hurt. So they keep pressing it and pressing it. Don't allow it to upset you. Don't allow it to phase you. Forget what they think. Seriously, forget it. They don't know your journey, where you've been or where you're heading

I recall a powerful story that I once heard about a man who was on a subway. He sat there on the subway, watching as a father was completely neglecting his three children. Two small boys and a little girl were simply out of control, and he was oblivious to the fact. He looked at the man in disdain. How could he ignore his children? How could he allow them to disrupt the subway ride for other passengers? Passengers who were too nice or to ambivalent to say anything.

Eventually, the man had stirred in his thoughts enough. He came to the end of his proverbial rope. He had to say something. Gripped with anger, he approached the father, asking him why he wasn't controlling his children. The man, looking back at him with a sorry face, apologized profusely. 'I know. I'm sorry. I guess I should do something, shouldn't I?' he asked. He fell silent for a moment and looked out the window of the moving subway car, towards the blackness on the other side, his eyes glazing over.

After a pause, he told the man what had happened. His wife had just died of cancer. They were coming back from the hospital. He was wondering what he was going to tell his kids or how he was going to explain it to them that their mother was gone forever. A solitary tear fell down the side of his face as the other passengers looked on in sorrow. 'I'm sorry,' said the man to the father. 'I had no idea.'

Trust your intuition and who you are deep down inside. One reason you absolutely shouldn't listen to the opinion of other people is because you should trust your intuition. You should trust who you are and why you're doing the things that you're doing. The most successful people in the world were ridiculed and shamed the most times for their dreams. How much do you think they were made fun of and scoffed at after failing over and over again?

The point is that you have to do what's right for you, and not base that decision on what other people think about you or what you're doing—nobody is perfect. Nobody has the right to declare you unfit or unworthy of something just because of a flaw or because you're different than others. As long as you're doing the right things in this world with the right motivations, it doesn't matter what other people's opinions are of you.

Keep light of the fact that many before you were judged, and many after you will continue to be judged. It will likely always be this way. That's the nature of a diverse society. We aren't all the same. And considering that fact, you shouldn't allow those opinions to affect you. At the end of the day, when we come to the end of this life, none of that will matter. What will matter will be our experiences and what value we brought to this world, not other people's opinions of us.

You will never please everyone with your decisions so don't try. It's impossible to please everyone. No matter what decision you make, someone is going to be upset. Someone is going to have an opinion of which path you follow or which direction you choose. They will judge you on what you do for your children, what you do for your career, what you do for your education, who your friends are, the places you spend your time, what you do for a living, and everything else in between.

How can you expect to please them all? How can you expect to appease and cater to the opinions of all those people out there who differ so widely from your views?

It's quite literally impossible. However, for one reason or another, we allow other people's opinions of us to dictate how we feel. When we make a decision, and people judge us negatively for it, we question whether or not we did the right thing.

Why? Why should it matter that we cater to others? They don't know you. They don't know all the things that you've been through. They don't know why you made that decision over another. So, why is their opinion the right opinion? It's not. It's subjective. Your decision is steeped in the present situation and circumstances that surround your life, not theirs. You're doing the best for you and your family. That's all that matters.

What's good for someone else might not be good for you. We are all so different. Everything about our lives is different. We're the product of different experiences, different upbringings, different values, and beliefs, and so on. So, doesn't that mean that what's good for someone else might not be good for you? Does it mean that there's some neat little box that all decisions go in? Does it mean that the opinion of the masses are correct and that they're justified in judging you? Of course it's not.

Yet, we base our sanity on those same opinions of others. We allow that to dictate how we feel at any given moment. Are we happy because someone approves of one of our decisions? Or, are we sad because others disapprove? Why should their opinion be the right opinion? Why should what's good for them, also be good for you? What is it about these negative people, and why do we allow it to so deeply affect us?

As long as we continue to give people the power and allow it to negatively affect us, they will continue to judge.

They will continue to say things to hurt us or make us feel unworthy of being in our own skins — that's not fair whatsoever. You should never do that to someone else and don't allow them to do it to you. You have to ignore that negativity. Chase your dreams and make your decisions based on what's good for you, not them.

Because taking the high road is always a better choice. God put us all here on the earth to thrive, not just to survive. Human beings were made to thrive. We were made to uplift others and make them feel good about themselves. Especially when they're trying to do the right thing in life and help their families, and add value to the world. No matter what anyone else says or thinks about you, taking the high road is always a better choice. Turn the other cheek, even if they have spit on both sides of your face already.

There's this universal oneness that binds us all. We are all the products of the same original energy in the universe produced nearly 14 billion years ago. Somehow, one way or another, we wound up in these human bodies, as conscious, and aware beings. And that energy is important. That energy dictates the sway and direction of your life. When chaneled properly, it can be an explosive power, one to create tremendous positivity in this world.

But that energy can also be used to reap sadness and sow animosity. Don't allow that to happen. Don't get sucked into negative thinking and people's poor opinions of you. It doesn't matter. Take the high road. Ignore the naysayers. Turn the other cheek no matter how much it burns you or hurts you inside to do so. At the end of the day, you'll be glad you did. You'll be glad you stayed in the realm of positivity rather than flinging yourself into the ring of negativity.

At a point, I eventually realized existing without ever truly living was not what I wanted for myself. So I made changes – I gradually embraced who I truly want to be and never looked back. If you are in the same place I once was – seeking approval from everyone for every little thing you do – please take this book to heart and start making changes today. Life is too short not to.

It's so easy to get so wrapped up in trying to be enough for everyone else that you begin to forget about what you want. Living up to other people's expectations can vary from not seeming like a big deal to feeling immense amounts of pressure to have a career and life your parents are proud of. Can I take a break from dating? Is my career path a huge mistake? Is something wrong with me? When you stop listening to everyone else and start following the path that feels right for you, there's a shift. Chances are it won't be perfect and might be a longer journey to get to where you want to go, but ultimately, I've found that the people I know who are doing what they want to do are much happier than the ones living for other people.

Things to Consider

First and foremost, you are not obligated to live up to everyone's expectations. Life is under no obligation to give us what we expect. And you are under no obligation to give others what they expect. Period. Do things because you care. Do things because you know it's right. Don't just do things because everyone else expects you to.

Expectations just get in the way of great life experiences. Don't let expectations (especially other people's expectations) get in your way. Truth be told, the unexpected is often better than the expected. Our entire lives can be described in one sentence: It didn't go as planned, and that's ok.

You don't need others to hold your hand every step of the way. Be willing to go alone sometimes. You don't need permission to grow. Not everyone who started with you will finish with you. And that's ok.

You get to learn from your mistakes without unnecessary third-party pressure. – You're going to mess up sometimes. But the good news is, as long as you're listening to your intuition, you get to decide how you're going to mess up. Which means you get to decide how you're going to live and what you're going to learn along the way.

No one knows you better than you know yourself. How you seem to others and how you actually are, rarely match. Even if they get the basic gist of who you are, they're still missing a big piece of the puzzle. What other people think of you will rarely contain the whole truth, which is fine. So, if someone forms an opinion of you based on superficialities, then it's up to them, not you, to reform those opinions. Leave it to them to worry about it. You know who you are and what's best for you.

Only YOU can define what's possible for you and your life. – Some people will kill you over time if you let them; and how they'll kill you is with tiny, harmless phrases like, "Be realistic." When this happens, close your ears and listen to your inner voice instead. Remember that real success in life isn't what others see, but how you feel. It's living your truth and doing what makes you feel alive. We've often heard the instructions of "turning the other cheek". Sometimes this can be extremely challenging; especially when you know that someone doesn't mean you any good. But it's crucial to turn the other cheek, even if they spit on both sides of your face. However, at some point you've got to know "when" is enough. As I mentioned earlier….. be realistic.

In the end, happiness is simply living your life your own way. There comes a time when your back is up against the wall and you realize all you can do is say, "Screw it, I'm doing things my way!" That's the earth-shattering moment you stop planning for someone else's expectations, and start making progress on what's truly important to YOU. That's when you begin to live life according to your own morals and values. That's when you can finally be at your happiest.

You can best serve yourself and others by giving yourself what YOU need. Don't ask yourself what the world needs, ask yourself what makes you come alive, and pursue it at all costs. That's what this world needs, people like YOU who come alive. Which means your needs matter; so don't ignore them. Sometimes you have to do what's best for you and your life, not just what seems best on the surface for everyone else.

Rather than being confined by opinions, you need to create your own reality. If J.K. Rowling stopped after being rejected by multiple publishers for years, there would be no Harry Potter. If Howard Schultz gave up after being turned down by banks 200+ times, there would be no Starbucks. If Walt Disney quit too soon after his theme park concept was trashed by 300+ investors, there would be no Disney World. One thing is for sure: If you give too much power to the opinions of others, you will become their prisoner. So never let someone's opinion define your reality.

You need to allow yourself the freedom to speak your truth. Yes, speak your truth even if your voice shakes. Be cordial and reasonable, of course, but don't tread carefully on every word you say. Push your concerns of what others might think aside. Let the consequences of doing so unravel naturally. What you'll find is that most of the time no one will be offended or irritated at all. And if they do get upset, it's likely only because you've started behaving in a way that makes them feel they have less power over you. Think about it. Why lie?

The wrong people should not be able to tamper with your standards. Remember, failed relationships aren't designed to encourage you to lower your standards, but to raise them and keep them up. So while you're out there making decisions instead of excuses, learning new things, and getting closer and closer to your goals, know that there are others out there, like me, who admire your efforts and are striving for greatness too. Bottom line: Don't let the wrong people bring you down.

The haters can have less of an effect on you. Don't worry about the haters, ever. Don't let them get to you. They're just upset because the truth you know contradicts the lies they live. Period.

Your individuality can be openly celebrated and enjoyed. Constantly seeking approval means you're perpetually worried that others are forming negative judgments of you. This steals the fun ingenuity, and spontaneity from your life. Flip the switch on this habit. If you're lucky enough to have something that makes you different from everybody else, don't be ashamed and don't change. Uniqueness is priceless. In this crazy world that's trying to make you like everyone else, find the courage to keep being your remarkable self. It takes a lot of courage to stand alone, but it's worth it. Being unapologetically YOU is worth it.

There can very easily be less drama to deal with on a daily basis. Forgo the drama. Ignore the negativity around you. Just be sincere and kind, and promote what you love instead of bashing what you hate.

You can create more time to socialize with the right people. When you're feeling insecure, you typically don't notice the hundreds of people around you who accept you just the way you are. All you notice are the few who don't. Don't ever forget your worth. Spend time with those who value you. No matter how good you are to people, there will always be negative minds out there who criticize you. Smile, ignore them and carry on. You might feel unwanted and unworthy to one person, but you are priceless to another.

Great relationships are not governed by one-sided expectations. When it comes to your relationships, don't keep everything you need to say to yourself. Let it out. Express your point of view. Communication is not just an important part of a relationship, communication is the relationship. Communicate even when it's uncomfortable and uneasy. One of the best ways to heal and grow a relationship is simply getting everything on the inside out in the open. Compromise. That's how good people make great things happen together.

You can be YOUR best without competing with everyone else. When you are happy to simply do your best and not compare or compete, everyone worth your while will respect you. Here are some healthy food for thought:

Always… Be strong, but not rude. Be kind, but not weak. Be humble, but not timid. Be proud, but not arrogant. Be bold, but not a bully.

You are not obligated to anyone more so than you are to yourself. Your relationship with yourself is the closest and most important relationship you will ever have. So don't forget about YOU out there, and don't be too hard on yourself either. There are plenty of others willing to do both for you. And remember, if you don't take good care of yourself, then you can't take good care of others either; which is why taking care of yourself is the best selfish thing you can do.

Notes

Notes

_____

_____

_____

_____

_____

_____

_____

_____

_____

_____

_____

_____

_____

_____

_____

_____

_____

_____

Chapter 3

What Type of People do You Attract?

Have you ever wondered why you attract the same type of people? Do you know why? Is it you that keep attracting the same type of people? Everything we attract on the outside is a reflection of what's inside. If you're trying to find a mate while you're still broken, you will attract a mate who is equally broken.

What you attract is a re-affirmation of what you believe. Your belief might have been influenced by past negative experiences that continue to stay with you for a while even after the relationship has ended and acts as a lens that you see the world through.

Until you change your belief, you will see everything and everyone through that lens and unconsciously try to select people who act in coherence with your belief. Unfortunately, this becomes a self-fulfilling prophecy of negative beliefs. Until you start to question your own beliefs and try to change them, you will unconsciously try to re-affirm that your beliefs are right.

This is why people who believe people cheat usually end up dating cheaters. Somewhere in their subconscious mind attracts the type that re-affirms their belief. If you look around at your friends, you would spot patterns. If you look at your past, you will spot patterns. Until you look deep into the hole within your heart, look at your upbringing and your relationship with parents, your attachment style, your values as well as the strengths that you are attracted that naturally come with the same set of weaknesses, you will never understand why you keep running into the same issues over and over. We gravitate towards the familiar more than right. We learned about love through our parents and by observing our parents.

When I was a child, I knew I had a large family and at the time, I felt they were all I needed but as I got older, I realized God wanted me to experience other relationships. As a person with a large family, you truly get tired of the same folks. One thing I realized about myself earlier was that I never wanted to be around a lot of people. I was a "loner" for the most part but for whatever reason, I was a very friendly child and always had a great personality. From elementary through middle school, I was very insecure and never felt I was attractive, so I tried to make it up by making sure I had a nice personality. The beauty of me was already inside of me and because of who I was. I was beginning to attract those that felt my sweet personality was a weakness, some saw the insecurity in me and there were those who could see that they could take me for granted because I was sheltered as a child. GOD made sure he placed the right people in my path, who would begin to mold the woman I was about to become.

You can change the pictures that make up your reality. You just have to be ready to acknowledge and most importantly, to release your limiting beliefs. Your inner blocks are lurking around in areas of your life where you are producing results you do not want. If you keep attracting certain people into your life or being in relationships you find unfulfilling, there are limiting beliefs that need to be released for you to experience a different, better reality. Control your inner state to control your reality.

Notes

Notes

_____

_____

_____

_____

_____

_____

_____

_____

_____

_____

_____

_____

_____

_____

_____

_____

_____

_____

Chapter 4

Recognizing the Toxic People

Are there toxic people in your life?

Perhaps you've experienced having that one fake friend who, when things are going well with your life, makes you feel like you're still not good enough by pointing out your flaws instead of affirming your success (for instance, someone who has a perpetual "crabs in a bucket mentality.") Or you might have a partner, or family member who makes you feel guilty about how great your life is. At the same time, they are struggling with their own lives claiming to be "victims" of a world that doesn't give them any breaks.

Do you feel drained, out of responses and advice for some of your Family and Friends? Do you know who the complainers are? Do you see the negative people around you? Is there a frown on your face when you get a call or visit for the individuals with such behaviors? What about the ones that are never happy or expecting you to make them happy? When you are younger, you aren't familiar with this behavior or when they begin to show the behavior of hurt, disappointment, and anger. You do not understand why hurt people hurt others. I have always shown kindness and love to all. I used to hear people tell me all the time how sweet I was. I would later hear more sweet loving words and compliments.

Not to say I was perfect and never had an attitude or issues because I did, However, most times, it was triggered by the actions of others. Being the oldest in my home, I was forced to do a lot. Some of the things my parents would ask me to do were so unfair. Such as, "clean up behind your brothers and sisters, you can't participate in activities because we need you to watch the kids", and so forth. These type of requests did bring about an attitude. I started having to care and be responsible for my siblings from the tender age of 8 until I was 17 years old. During this age period of my life, I had also experienced the journey of many friendships. Which helped me mold into the woman I have become. A woman that I can honestly say, never set out to hurt, plot, steal, boss, control, or make anyone's lives miserable.

Actions bring about a reaction; whether it's good or bad. Toxic people are the ones that are damaged through bad life experiences. Statistics show that most toxic people who grow up in dysfunctional homes. My home was not perfect at all, but I made a choice in my life that I did not want to be someone who was a problem to anyone. I pride myself on always being friendly to everyone. I was raised in that environment. However, as I journeyed through my life with family and friends, I learned that some were not as privileged to grow up the same. Eventually, this reality seemed to have caused a chain reaction in my life with other friends as well.

Types of Toxic People

First, let's describe a toxic person. This is anyone whose behavior adds negativity and upset to your Life. Many times, toxic people are dealing with their stresses and traumas. To do this, they act in ways that don't present them in the best light and usually upset others along the way.

After many years of family and friendship experiences, it became easier to identify the toxic people. Do you have them around you?

Narcissist – This is a person who has an excessive interest or admiration of themselves. This person thinks the world revolves around them. What does this kind of individual do? A narcissistic personality disorder involves a pattern of self-centered, arrogant thinking and behavior, a lack of empathy for others people, and an excessive need for admiration. This type of person is cocky, manipulative, selfish, patronizing, and demanding.

The Follower – This is someone who supports and is guided by another person in a group.

The Faker – This person takes an action with the intent to deceive. He/She is not genuine and will do whatever it takes to make themselves look good.

Mr. or Ms. Perfect – This is an individual who believes they are excellent and always correct and they could do no wrong.

The Jealous – This person feels resentment against someone because of that person's rivalry, success or advantages.

The Church Lady – The female who is actively involved in the church and acts upright and uptight. She is judgmental and portrays an image as if she has never done anything wrong in her life.

Negative – This person tends to be downbeat, disagreeable, skeptical and has a pessimist attitude that always expects the worst.

Mr. & Mrs. Better than You – He or she feels superior to someone else.

The Controller – This individual tries to control others or situations. They have the behavior to assert dominance.

The Bitter – This is an individual who holds grudges, is often jealous, and generally focuses on the dark side of Life.

The Blame person – This is an individual who holds everyone responsible for something negative that happens to them; they never see themselves at fault.

The Gossiper – This individual talks eagerly and casually about other people. Someone who enjoys spreading rumors and hears the latest news about others such as Family and Friends.

The Beggar – A person who lives by asking others for gifts, things, and whatever they can get.

The Bossy – This is someone who gives orders and who wants things his/her ways. Example: Always telling others what to do.

The Conniving - Is someone prone to scheme in a harmful way. Example: A person who is always scheming to take things that don't belong to him or her.

The Theft – Someone who takes something that doesn't belong to them. Example: At a birthday party, you left your purse on the table, your so-call friend decides to quietly pick it up and walk away with it.

The Scammer – An individual who commits or participates in a fraudulent scheme or operation.

The Liar – Is a person who never speaks the truth.

The Trifling – Is someone dishonest, shady, secretive, a player, all talk without following through.

The Territorial – One who guards or defends an area she considers to belong to her.

Characteristics Exhibited by Toxic People

You or others are blamed for the negative feelings and circumstances in their life. Toxic people tend to project their feelings of inadequacy or insecurity towards the people closest to them rather than be accountable for these emotions. For example, someone who is in a bad mood but won't own their feelings or take responsibility for them may turn to you and say, "You're sure in a bad mood today," which will probably leave you confused. You'll often find yourself on the defense without really understanding why. You will get accusations or questions that don't make any sense to you or seemingly come out of nowhere.

You are wrong and they are right all the time.

When someone in your life does not admit mistakes and insists that you are wrong all the time, you're likely dealing with a toxic person. They will go to great extremes to be right, including changing facts or challenging your memories. Toxic people do not readily admit when they have made a mistake, miscalculated something, or misspoken.

They disregard your boundaries.

It does not matter if you've requested that they stop behaving a certain way, a toxic person will continue to behave in a way that violates your wishes. Toxic people will also expect you to come through for them regardless of the time of day and your circumstance. It's almost impossible to build a positive and supportive relationship with people who disregard your boundaries. Also, you don't even recognize when they're walking all over you. Your boundaries are the barriers that you set to separate yourself from the world around you. Your boundaries help define you and ensure that you are protected from people who are hurtful, disrespectful, and invasive. People with the healthy boundaries know their limits and can express themselves. However, people with unhealthy boundaries pull on you in aggressive ways and don't know when to stop.

They are habitually dishonest.

Toxic people are known for their constant lies, even if they are about the smallest things. This could be a matter of exaggerating the facts of a story or truly making something up, a common manipulative tactic used by gaslighters. They might do it because they have very low self-esteem and they are trying to give it a boost, or perhaps it's their way of getting what they want. If a toxic person is telling you an elaborate story, you can typically assume that it is only a half-truth.

They don't apologize.

Even if they are wrong, toxic people will usually not apologize. On instances when toxic people do apologize, it's usually a calculated move to manipulate you to give them what they want. They always feel like they have to be right, no matter what and will change the information to be right, or blame other people.

They revel in being victims.

Their victim status is a manipulative strategy to gain sympathy and attention. Toxic people can always find someone else to blame for their problems. Maybe they missed a deadline because no one reminded them about it, or they are late for work because their spouse didn't set an alarm. Bad things happen to everyone at some point. However, toxic people are happy to blame everyone else for their problems, including the problems they should take ownership of. But chances are, whatever happens to a toxic person will be someone else's fault.

They are habitually sarcastic.

A little bit of sarcasm here and there can be funny. However, too much sarcasm can hurt people's feelings and belittle them. Hence, it's a favorite weapon of toxic people. Sarcasm is rooted in anger, distrust, and weakness. Toxic people are so used to communicating with sarcasm that they can't see how much damage they're doing. When called out on it, toxic people often respond to the accusation of being hurtful with even more anger. Excessive sarcasm is never a healthy way to communicate with people.

They refuse to listen to you.

Toxic people act bored or change the conversation topic when you are talking. However, they expect you to listen to them when they're the ones talking. Your talking takes away any attention that could be on them and puts the focus on you. Recognize the signs of toxic people and learn how to deal with a toxic person. Toxic people disregard your boundaries even after you've requested that they stop behaving a certain way. Rather than listening to what you have to say to understand you, a toxic person will only be thinking of what they want to say next. They will seem uninterested in what you have to say and will turn the conversation back to themselves instead of trying to understand where you are coming from.

They feign concern for your welfare.

Pretending they are concerned about you is a ploy that toxic individuals often use to make you feel like they care about you, especially when you are beginning to sense that something is off. This false sense of concern can be mistaken for genuine remorse, but it is just a calculated attempt to catch you at a weak moment or appeal to your sentimentality. Toxic people will suck you back into the relationship by showing you desirable behaviors as soon as they think you are about to wiggle your way free from their grip. Remember, you deserve better.

They are critical of others.

You will notice that toxic people habitually put others down. If you are with someone who is constantly speaking poorly about others when those people are not around, chances are that they are doing the same to you. Toxic people are likely to harp on the weaknesses that they see in others to boost their self-esteem. They will verbally judge people for superficial things or harp on someone's honest mistake, and rarely point out the good in people.

They make you feel defensive about your decisions.

Everything you say or do is met with argument, and you begin to wonder if this person is questioning your intelligence. The criticisms and sarcasm directed at you can eventually take their toll and keep you on your guard. What behaviors are indicators that a person is toxic and how to deal with toxic people? Toxic people act bored or change the conversation topic when you are talking but expect you to listen to them when they're the ones talking. You stop feeling like you can be yourself around this person in anticipation of them criticizing you and eventually find yourself filtering what you say when you're conversing with a negative person.

They are inconsistent in their behavior.

Nothing is stable when you're with a toxic person. Opinions, preferences, and plans could go one way today and another way tomorrow. Often, there isn't an obvious explanation of the change in attitude, you can just tell something isn't right. They might be cold or cranky, and when asked if something's wrong, they say "nothing", but they'll add in a sigh or a facial expression to let you know that something is going on. You then probably look for ways to make them happy, which is why toxic people do this. Toxic people know that decent people will go out of their way to keep the people around them happy. They realize that you are uncomfortable wondering what they're thinking. However, you shouldn't have to constantly guess which version of the person you will be interacting with each day.

They have no interest in what's important to you.

Instead, they will find a reason why your good news isn't so great. For example, if you are about to go on a trip to the beach, they might say, "The heat is going to be miserable." Or, if you just got a promotion at work, they might say, "That's a huge amount of work for such little compensation." Talking about the good things happening in your life takes away the spotlight from them, so toxic friends or family members often use fault-finding to make you feel inferior. If you are excited that something amazing just happened to you, you are often better off keeping it to yourself when you are around toxic people.

They boast about their achievements.

The need to brag has its roots in deep-seated insecurity.

People who feel inferior spend their time overcompensating to make themselves appear to be superior to others. The only way these uncertain people can be happy is by making other people noticeably unhappy. Toxic people often brag about compensating for the shortcomings that they desperately hope you will never discover. Toxic people gossip and use effective ways to deal with them. A toxic person gossips about you and talks behind your back. For them, everyone else is awful or lacking in some way. They will even take credit for someone else's accomplishments because they need the validation to feel like they are better than others. These people who have no sense of self-worth still have an intrinsic need to feel like a valuable member of society, and this need can only be met if they project their perceived greatness.

They take, take, and take.

As long as you're able or willing, toxic people will take from you; your time, possessions, and attention without consideration or any thought of returning or giving back what they've taken. This is a form of manipulation. When you are with this person, you likely feel like you are the only one who is contributing to the relationship. Toxic people send a message that you owe something to them — and chances are, you believe it. They are even able to take from you or hurt you in some way and then insist they did it all for you. This is especially common in relationships where there is some differentiation in power, such as in a working relationship. For example, a supervisor may say, "I've left this three months worth of filing for you. I figured that you would appreciate the experience of learning how to use the filing cabinets" or, "I'm hosting a dinner party — why don't you bring the food? It'll allow you to show off your cooking skills."

If you have any of these types of toxic people in your life, "RUN" as soon as you can. These types of people will play a major impact on your life in a not-so-good light in your life. Although you may not be this person or do anything such as this, knowing who does and having them in your life will not be good for you; they will always be distractions to where you are going.

Notes

Notes

Notes

Chapter 5

How to Remove Yourself from Distractors

By now you have concluded that a lot of time has been wasted dealing with the various toxic folks in your life who have caused you hurt, disappointments, bad arguments, drama, and continuations of negativity and toxins. Perhaps, you have reflected on all the years that were wasted trying to help those who did not want or need help; or those you've helped only to learn that it was never enough. Many times your goals and dreams were delayed because you allowed those family and friends to keep interrupting your journey towards your purpose. You allowed them to distract you and cause your purpose to be delayed and placed on hold.

Earlier, you didn't know who they were until they began to reveal themselves to you. Now that you have identified the toxic people who are your family and friends, how do you remove them?

I was that person. I struggled for years not knowing how to remove toxic people from my inner world because I still cared and loved them. This is when God reminds you "He is God". I started praying. I asked him to remove those who were not supposed to be in my Life, inner circle, and around me. A lot of times when we pray to God, we are expecting Him to give us what we want. Most times, God is always going to provide us with what is best.

When God showed me the list of people to remove from my life, I wasn't shocked at all. You see, there are lot of things you know already but you go into denial. Many of us had already received warnings about these individuals, but like most humans we ignore it until we keep finding ourselves in the same position (unhappy, exhausted, and stressed out about the burden they continue to place on us).

Once my "God-approved" list was clear to me, I started seeing, one by one, that some of the toxic people were beginning to act out. I had become bold enough to address it as I had done in the past; but this time I was stronger. I was also confident and assured that I did not want these individuals in my inner circle. Did I still love them? Yes, but we can love anyone with prayers and from a distance. This confidence did not grow overnight, but once God showed me who was not meant to be in my life anymore or belong to my inner circle, I was ok. The saying is, "If God Is for you, who can be against you?" Once I acted on the instructions from GOD, I was beginning to get my life back and I was now back on my journey to my purpose.

However, acting out the verdict of God may not be as easy as just hearing it and acting it out. The bible recorded that wisdom is profitable to direct. Removing these sets of people from your life requires wisdom, and below is a set of tips you can apply to remove these toxic people from your life.

Be firm.

"Toxins have to be met with a powerful force. It's likely that they won't just respond to 'Go away,' and will perhaps even dig their claws in deeper if you try to create a separation. Don't let this discourage you." Be very, very clear with the person about your intentions, then keep the necessary distance to make sure your message isn't misconstrued.

Set boundaries.

And stick with them. Stick with your boundaries long-term or [toxic people] will use any weakness overtime to sneak back into your life. If you told yourself you wouldn't respond to their texts, don't. Block their number and block them on all social media. Don't send them any e-mails and don't check in six months from now. Once you've decided to end a relationship, you're responsible for keeping the guidelines clear after the fact.

Don't be too nice.

It may sound harsh, but since toxic people tend to take advantage of any kindness that's imparted to them, being overly nice can be detrimental. "Realize that they get their energy from draining your loving and good nature. They thrive on your trust and kindness. It doesn't mean you have to be cruel (to paraphrase Michelle Obama, when they go low, you want to go high), but you should stop going out of your way to being overly accommodating.

Realize it's not your job to save them.

Toxic people are great at showing up when they need something, particularly during crisis moments in their own lives. They'll ask for a shoulder to cry on or an ear for you to lend. They may disguise it as wanting advice. All of these are ploys for your time and attention. Do not give in to them, no matter the circumstance.

If things are truly dire for your friend, you can direct him to resources that specialize in his particular issues. Solving his problems is not only not your responsibility; it's likely beyond your capabilities.

Know that when it's done; it's done.

Toxic people will keep coming back if you let them, so when you decide to say goodbye, make sure you're ready to make it permanent. They will always find a way to create a problem or drama in your life. When you've decided to move on, move on for good.

If the toxic person is family, and it's therefore impossible to make a clean break, you can still establish clear limits for your interactions (be it, we will only speak on the phone once a month or you will only visit during the holidays).

Treat your separation like the breakup it is.

Yes, we need relationships, but we don't need every relationship, especially ones that bring us more pain than support. Energy flows where attention goes. The more selective you are about where your focus is, the more successful you'll be. The more time you spend away from toxic people, the more time you have for yourself and the people that are positive, uplifting, and important to you. Make time for people who bring you happiness, and let go of those who bring you anything less.

Who Should be in Your Inner Circle of Family/Friends?

By now, you should have identified the ones you know who are imperative to keep in your life due to the history of your friendship with family and friends. After I evaluated the relationships I had with both family and friends (all the ups and down). I decided who were the supportive ones, the individuals who had my back when my back was turned, the individuals that were respectful, loyal, kind, loving, sweet as I was and the ones who came into my life just as I was; "Like-Minded."

Finally, I am so happy with this part of my life. I have combined those family members, childhood friends, college friends, colleagues and friends who I met throughout my life. I've also narrowed down who is supposed to be in my inner circle. This is a fresh of breath air for me in my life because I can now continue where I left off without the "toxicity" involved. Although, the ones I left behind still remain my family and friends. Though I continue to love them, this does not mean that all I have for them is hatred. It doesn't mean I don't care for them or that I hold any animosity. All it meant is that I decided what was best for my life. The weight of their issues, problems, and hidden agenda caused a major distraction in my world and because of that, I had to do what was important for me.

Notes

Notes

Notes

_____

_____

_____

_____

_____

_____

_____

_____

_____

_____

_____

_____

_____

_____

_____

_____

_____

Chapter 6

Quantity or Quality?

Life is not about the quantity of friends you have, but about the quality of those friends.

Eventually, after years of experience with people, you learn which individuals remain in touch based on how strong the relationship is; the ones with whom you weathered the storms, the ones you can convince to no longer cause a delay or distraction on your way. As you mature, you do realize that some family and friends become different and their individual lives do change. My life was not perfect but in this world on earth, you will experience change, growth, and clarity of seasons with others. After so many ups and downs and distraction in your life, the list of your family and friends will get smaller.

My distractions were merely from those I allowed to enter and cause a major delay. As you journey through friendships, you will realize that quality is better than quantity. Over the years, I have become close to my family and gained many friends throughout my life. Once you go through seasons of people, you discover that having many friends was just in numbers but not in quality. Many of them do not deserve to be in your life.

Let's break down the two components:

Quantity

Because of who I am, my personality is big. I am fun, I love to laugh, dance, and be that one person you can count on to give you positive messages. I was the person who had many family and friends. They filled up my house parties, birthdays, celebrations and various events. However, those things did not satisfy my heart. There are some family and friends layered around you who appear to be for you. Some of them wear masks and until the masks comes off in layers, you will not see the true face.

Quality

After many years of dealing with toxic people, I now discovered what type of people I prefer and deserve in my life. The long list has now been shortened to a few people. You must be confident of the quality of family and friends you deserve to have in your life. Qualities I look for in my circle of friends are listed below:

Positive
Caring
Inspiring
Patient
Respect
Love
Comforting
Present
Supportive
Commitment

Notes

_____

_____

_____

_____

_____

_____

_____

_____

_____

_____

_____

_____

_____

_____

_____

_____

_____

_____

_____

Notes

_____

_____

_____

_____

_____

_____

_____

_____

_____

_____

_____

_____

_____

_____

_____

_____

_____

Conclusion

Once I discovered what prevented me from my purpose and accomplishing my goals, I was so excited and determined to continue where I left off. Now that I have finally removed the distractors and returned them to their proper place, I am now beginning to move closer to my purpose. Going through the process of clearing out toxic people (who were major parts of my distractions) was a breakthrough in what affected me mentally. When your mind is filled with your problems and the problems of others, it is very hard to stay on your path. You must take charge of your life and avoid people or things that will prevent you from your purpose.

You Are Designed To Thrive: Experience the Amazing Benefits of Knowing GOD and having the Right Type of People in Your Life. When God created us, he knew all of us would be born with a purpose in life. I believe we are to experience the education of people's behavior to deal with challenges on our journey to our purpose. All of us are designed to thrive, but it is up to us to remove those things that are in the way, preventing us from thriving. Never feel guilty about focusing on what God has called you to do. Never feel guilty about removing those things that are in your way to get there.

Today, I am progressing through life, planning my retirement, focusing on my business and celebrating the completion of my first book (the one you just read!). Currently, I have a happy balanced life and a world of quality friends who do not distract me from my purpose and fully respect and support my dreams.

In conclusion, please remember, "You Can't Change People, Just Change How You Deal with Them" so that you can accomplish what God has planned for you in this life.

You Have Arrived...

1. Have you identified your Distractors?

2. Do you know the impact the Distractors have on your Life?

3. Have you calculated the time you have lost dealing with unnecessary Distractors?

4. What is your plan to eliminate the Distractors?

5. During this exercise what have you learned about yourself and Distractors?

_____

_____

_____

_____

_____

_____

_____

_____

_____

_____

Weekly Reminders to Self!

Live For You!

Uniqueness is Priceless!

You Are the Artist of Your Life!

Stop Giving Power to Others!

Create Value and Contribution to The World!

Your Self-Worth Isn't Defined by An Approval Rating!

Don't Live Up to Everyone Expectation!

Trust Your Own Intuition!

Nobody Has the Right to Declare You Unfit or Unworthy!

Do Not Let the Opinion of Others Affect You!

You Are Designed to Thrive!

Don't Get Sucked into Negative Thinking and People's Poor Opinions of You!

Stop Seeking Approval from Everyone!

Embrace Who You Want To Be!

Follow The Path That Feels Right for You!

Don't Judge Me!

Progress Not Perfection!

Know Your Worth!

What are Your Favorite Quotes?

ANTICIPATE THE NEXT BOOK RELEASE IN 2023/2024!

Glass In the Grass

Wait One Minute

Thank you for your support!

-Gerri

About the Author

Geraldine Holmes

Driven by a strong predilection to impact other people's lives positively and to fulfill her desire to be published, Geraldine Holmes is an avid author who writes relatable content with both men and women being at the center of her non-fiction writing journey. Her writing works are mostly based on day-to-day real-life experiences, making her a rare and resourceful gem in helping her audience handle such experiences. As a flexible and adaptive individual, she is a self-taught dancer, event planner/coordinator, a soloist and a Public Health Advisor.

In her debut title, Distractions, Geraldine underlines the significance of one's purpose. She stresses the essence of denying toxic people a chance to take it away. She does this expertly by ruling out vulnerability to bow down to the needs of unhealthy people in her readers' lives despite the closeness they share with them. Primarily, she strives to send a wake-up call to her readers, motivating them to adjust and effect vital changes in life to live their purpose to its level best.

In a highly skillful manner, Geraldine gears every chapter of her book Distractions towards exploring some awareness and identification of the type of people in her readers' lives and emotions that play a crucial role in identifying unhealthy characters. She helps her readers distinguish difficult and toxic people, learn when to walk away from toxicity, remaining tender in unhealthy relationships, developing inner strength, and investing in reliable people. Based on her experience, she offers herself to give the best advice to help others build self-love, focus on freedom from toxic people and achieve overall growth in life.

Currently, Geraldine lives in Stone Mountain, GA, with her family. Whenever she is not absorbed in the fast-paced work life, she enjoys dancing, convening parties for friends and family, singing, watching old and new movies, socializing and dancing. Upon her retirement, she plans to become a business owner, write more books and a traveler for adventure and exploration. She is passionate about God, giving, and helping people live better lives free from distractions.